DECORATIVE PAPERS & FABRICS

DECORATIVE PAPERS & FABRICS

ANNETTE HOLLANDER

Van Nostrand Reinhold Company
New York Cincinnati Toronto London Melbourne

Van Nostrand Reinhold Company Regional Offices:
New York Cincinnati Chicago Millbrae Dallas
Van Nostrand Reinhold Company International Offices:
London Toronto Melbourne

Designed by Joan Ann Jacobus
Printed by Halliday Lithograph Corp.
Color printed by Toppan Printing Co., Ltd.

Published by Van Nostrand Reinhold Company
450 West 33rd Street, New York, N.Y. 10001
Published simultaneously in Canada by
Van Nostrand Reinhold Ltd.
16 15 14 13 12 11 10 9 8 7 6 5 4 3 2 1

TO BILL

CONTENTS

PREFACE

In her Introduction to *Decorative Papers and Fabrics,* Annette Hollander writes that she is presenting "new approaches to design techniques," that these techniques depend upon "spontaneity." This is understatement, and inadequately calls attention to the book's unique merits.

Mrs. Hollander has developed the six new techniques for decorating paper and fabric described in this book, simplifying, modernizing, and "cross-breeding" old methods of marbling, starch papers, fold and dye, wax resist, potato printing. Use of these techniques, Mrs. Hollander points out, produces "happenings," designs that are always accidental, limitless in number, and infinitely satisfying to the creative impulse.

Studies by psychologists suggest how fundamental is the need to satisfy the creative impulse. These go beyond the common recognition of the importance of self-expression in an industrialized urban society. Many psychologists infer—from observing chimpanzees' involvement with their paintings, children's use of earth, sand, floors, and walls on which to make designs and pictures, the therapeutic gain by the emotionally ill from opportunities to work in the arts and crafts—that creativity produces a gratification based on the need to affect the environment, to place one's mark or imprint on the world.

Ideas coming from recent research in the psychology of the arts seem even more pertinent to underscoring the merits of Mrs. Hollander's book. Art, these investigations suggest, jolts us out of our necessarily ordered patterns of perceiving and behaving, and gives us a chance to prepare ourselves for new situations and complexities. Some confirmation of this theory comes from another avenue psychologists are now taking. Personality studies have indicated that artists and those who are most attracted to art are more willing and able than most other people to be flexible, to accept complexities and ambiguities.

A book that encourages spontaneity, that gives explicit and simple ways to practice facing the accidental and to recognize the infinite varieties of the possible not only has merit, but is essential. At the moment, no other book presents the techniques Mrs. Hollander has devised. And the techniques, it should be noted, can be adapted for use by everyone from the kindergarten child to the skilled craftsman.

All of this states solemnly what can be said simply. Mrs. Hollander's clear, easy-to-follow explanations of new ways to design fabric and paper make for fun and excitement.

Rosaline S. Schwartz
Assistant Instructor, Psychology of the Arts
Yale University

INTRODUCTION

This book contains new approaches to design techniques for decorating papers and fabrics that are old, but rarely used today. Since the techniques are easy and inexpensive, and produce a design in a very brief time, they may be enjoyed by young children as well as by adults with no previous experience.

Although the results of beginning experimentation with the basic techniques are usually almost purely accidental, such results, owing to the nature of the techniques, are surprisingly beautiful. Inspiration for a deliberate print might arise from such an accidental design. Once one becomes familiar with a technique, he may expect to be more selective, to achieve some control over the results of his work, and to succeed in balancing colors and shapes as he chooses. Experience will also suggest some variation of the basic techniques; samples of some possible variations are presented in the text.

The fresh and charming quality of the decorative papers and fabrics depends upon one very necessary ingredient: spontaneity. And spontaneity is assured, for the inexpensive materials employed may be used freely, and successful results are the rule rather than the exception.

1. MARBLED PAPERS & FABRICS

Marbling, an old design technique of unknown origin, is used to produce patterns on paper or fabric that are similar in appearance to marble. Marbled designs, such as 1-1, are prints that are transferred to paper or fabric from patterns of ink suspended on a solution, known as a size, of water and Carrageen moss extract.

First, the size must be prepared, starting twenty-four hours before it is to be used. Carrageen moss, or Irish moss (1-2), as it is sometimes called, is a form of alga that is tan or light brown in color. It may be found along rocky coastlines, or it may be purchased from sources listed in the back of the book. The size is prepared by boiling a cup of moss in two quarts of water for three minutes. Two cups of cold water are then added. After the resulting mixture has been left standing at room temperature for twenty-four hours, it is strained through cloth (a terry-cloth towel is convenient) to remove the large particles. The size is then ready for use. It will give good results for three or four days, after which it should be discarded. Fresh size may be prepared in large quantities, frozen, and then thawed as it is needed.

Oil-base block-printing ink, etching ink, printers' ink, and artists' oil colors may be used alone or in combination for marbling. These colors should be diluted with a little paint thinner, but not turpentine, before use. When a very thick ink such as printers' ink is used, a paint spatula or palette knife is useful for mixing the ink and thinner thoroughly on a piece of glass.

1-2

1-3

1-4

The paper on which the prints are made may be of any kind, white or colored, as long as it does not have a glossy finish.

The strained solution of moss extract is poured into a shallow pan for printing. The pan may be lined with kitchen plastic wrap so that it will not become soiled, and a piece of white paper may be placed under the wrap at the bottom of the pan so that the colors and patterns in the size may be seen clearly. Before printing, the surface tension of the solution is broken by drawing a piece of newspaper across the surface.

When a steel nail is dipped in ink and then touched to the surface of the size, the drop usually spreads on the size into a circle (1-3). The nail may then be used to draw through several such circles of color, forming a pattern (1-4). It is best that the nail just skim the surface of the solution.

1-5

The paper to which the pattern on the size is to be transferred is held at diagonally opposite corners, lowered into the size, and then released, as shown in 1-5. This procedure prevents air pockets from forming under the paper. When the paper is lifted from the solution, the pattern on the surface of the liquid will have been transferred to the paper. The paper is then rinsed or blotted with a paper towel or sponge, and set aside to dry. The pattern on the paper will not smear, unless an excessive amount of ink has been suspended on the size.

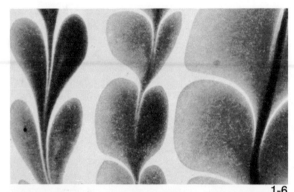

1-6

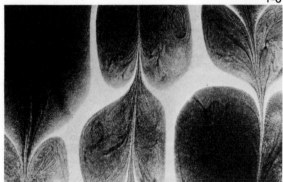

1-7

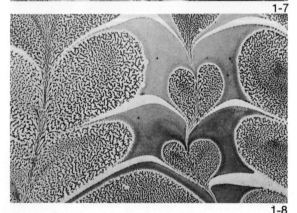

1-8

Before a second pattern is attempted on the size, a piece of newspaper should be used to pick up remaining traces of ink from the size. The newspaper is laid on the size in the same manner used for transferring marbled patterns.

A nail was drawn downwards through columns of drops in 1-6. The clean lines of this print were obtained by the use of printers' ink. In 1-7, a nail was drawn down the first column of drops, up the second, and down the third. The block-printing ink used for this pattern typically spreads in such a way that the finished pattern appears to have translucent veins in it.

Two colors of ink were used in 1-8. The unusual texture of the darker ink is one of the unpredictable accidents that can occur in this medium, depending upon the kind of ink used, the order in which the inks and colors are used, the age of the size, and atmospheric conditions. Colors spread best when black ink is used as the first color to be dropped on the size.

After drops of ink had spread on the surface of the solution in 1-9, a second drop of another color was placed in the center of each. The second set of drops did not spread, which accounts for the tonal contrast in the resulting pattern. The pattern was then traced with a nail in the paths illustrated in 1-10 and 1-11. The pattern in 1-12 was made by dropping only one color on the size and then tracing with a nail in the same manner.

1-9

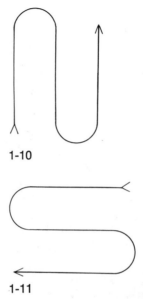

1-10

1-11

1-12

1-13

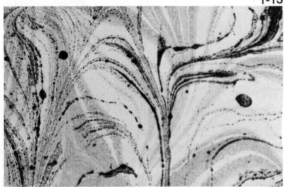

1-14

1-15

After a print has dried, it may be used to pick up a second pattern from the size. The second pattern in 1-13, printed horizontally, was much the same as the original vertical pattern. In 1-14, a pattern in dark ink was printed over a pale pattern.

Swirls with very fine lines are made by tracing through the ink with a needle rather than a nail; 1-15 is an example.

The prints in 1-16 and 1-17 were made as follows: Several colors of ink were suspended on the size, and the nail was drawn horizontally back and forth through these rows (in the manner illustrated in 1-18). Then a specially made comb was drawn vertically through the pattern. Such a comb (1-19) is made by cutting a row from a paper of pins, and taping the row of pins to a piece of cardboard. Every other pin was removed from the comb illustrated. The use of a comb usually produces a different effect from repeated parallel strokes of a needle, because the lines made by the comb are evenly spaced, as shown in 1-20 and 1-21. The comb was moved erratically over the surface of the solution in 1-22, 1-23, and 1-24. In 1-25 some of the pins of the comb were removed, at odd intervals, before the comb was moved over the surface of the solution. No pins were removed from the comb used in making the pattern in 1-26, so that the lines are very close together.

Feathery effects, such as those in 1-27 and 1-28, are achieved with an upward stroke of the comb (1-29) through the arcs of a pattern made by rows of overlapping drops of color, as illustrated in 1-16.

1-27

1-28

1-29

1-30

It has been shown that some inks have a great propensity for spreading, and that, in doing so, they push more sluggish inks aside. Gold oil-base block-printing ink, when diluted with paint thinner, spreads very readily and etches into all other inks, pushing them into thin lines of concentrated color. These thin, concentrated lines may be traced into a delicate pattern (1-30). The gold color usually does not transfer to the paper, and is therefore often useful for dispersing ink in the event that an excessive amount has been accidentally suspended on the size. Another example of the use of gold is in 1-31.

Marbling can be used to decorate the edges of a pad of paper (1-32). The pad is barely touched to the surface of the solution, while the edges of the pad are pressed tightly together with the fingers (1-33). Submerging the pad will cause the size to run up between the sheets of paper and ruin the pad. Excess size should be wiped off the pad with a dry cloth before it is set aside to dry. A weight on the pad while it is drying helps to keep the edges of the pages flat. Instructions for making the pad cover are given in the back of the book.

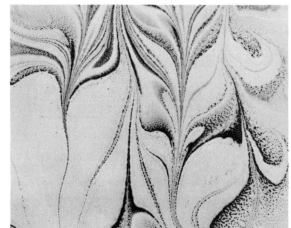

1-31

1-32

1-33

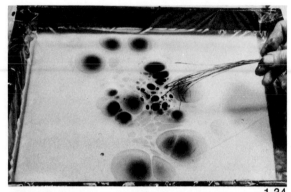

1-34

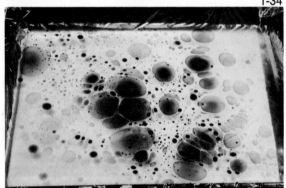

1-35

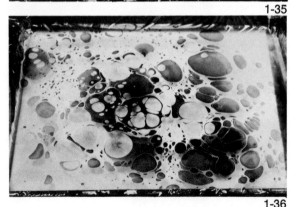

1-36

A small stiff brush or a bundle of straws from a broom tied together with a rubber band may be dipped in ink and tapped while held over the surface of the solution, so that droplets of color fall in a random fashion (1-34). Because subsequent splatters of ink do not spread as much, they form smaller circles of color (1-35). In 1-36, a second color, red, which was thrown on black droplets with a separate set of straws, etched into the black. A nail drawn through the pattern produced the effect in 1-37. Further examples of color thrown in this fashion are shown in 1-38, 1-39, and 1-40.

Highly irregular patterns can be produced deliberately. For example, picking up a print with trembling hands, or jarring the solution pan while picking up a print, produces a pattern with a turbulent appearance (1-41). Another sort of distorted pattern was made by violently tipping the solution pan just before transferring the pattern to the paper (1-42).

The addition of too much water to the moss solution is generally ill-advised because it is then difficult to produce controlled patterns. Nevertheless, these uncontrolled patterns can sometimes be quite graceful and interesting, as is the one in 1-43.

Marbling may also be done on water instead of on size; in this case also, control is minimal (1-44). When water is used as size, combs and nails are of no use, but the spreading ink may be manipulated to an extent by gentle coaxing with the edge of a piece of paper.

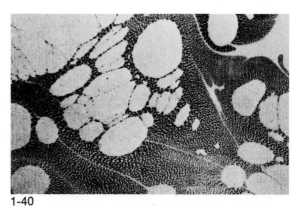

1-40

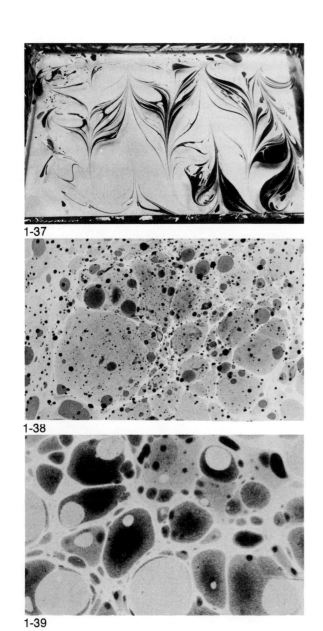

1-37

1-38

1-39

1-41

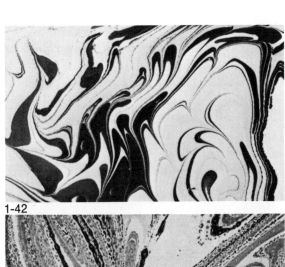

1-42

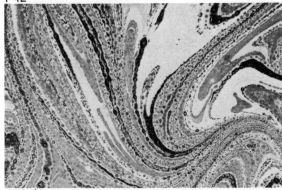

1-43

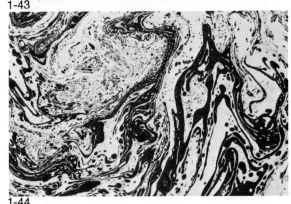

1-44

27

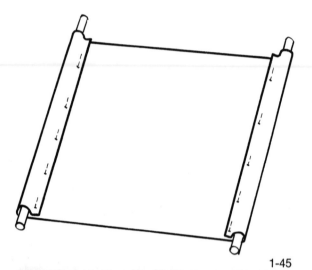

1-45

1-46

Fabric rather than paper may be used for marbling (C-1). The procedure is the same as for paper, except that the ends of larger pieces of fabric may be pinned to dowels at each end to ease lowering the material into the size (1-45). The fabric must remain on the liquid until it is saturated so that the entire reverse side of the fabric is wet, or the pattern will not adhere. The fabric is then rinsed in warm water to remove the size and is hung to dry.

Marbling on burlap is shown in 1-46, on cotton in 1-47. The bow tie in 1-48 was marbled on cotton material with a single color. The draw-string bag in 1-49 was marbled on linen.

Marbling with fabric may be done on water as well as on size, with the uncontrolled effect shown in 1-50.

Examples of fabric marbled on a thin solution of starch water, which is more readily available than moss, are shown in 1-51 and 1-52. Starch water is prepared as follows: A paste is made with cold water and corn starch in a sauce pan. Boiling water is added a little at a time and the mixture is cooked until the solution is thin, but not so thin that the marbling cannot be controlled. This will take experimentation. This size is not as satisfactory as that of Irish moss, because it is more difficult to control.

1-48

1-49

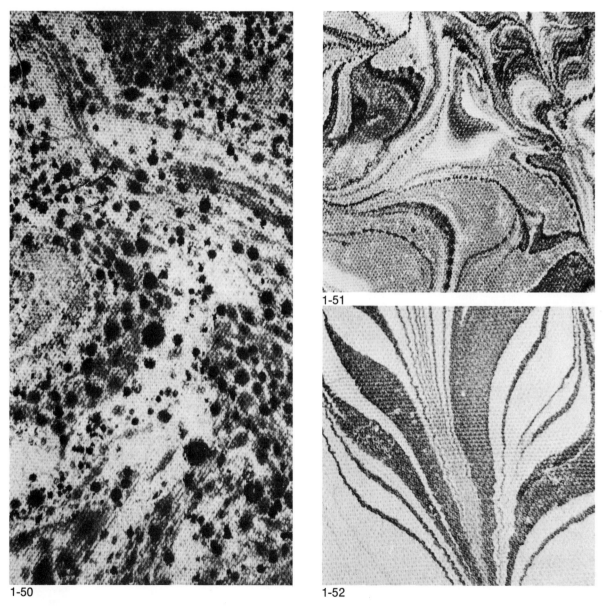

1-50

1-51

1-52

2. FOLD & DYE PAPERS

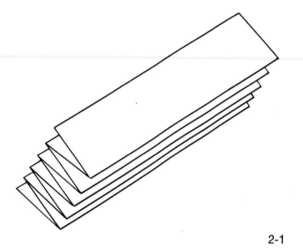

2-1

The fold-and-dye technique for decorating papers (C-2), which utilizes no special materials other than rice paper and food coloring, is basically simple, yet it produces many special effects, some being rather oriental in quality, others having the appearance of stained glass. The procedure consists essentially of folding rice paper into a small, compact rectangle or triangle and dipping the corners and edges of the figure into the food coloring.

Rice paper is a soft, absorbent paper that can be purchased in a variety of sizes and weights. It is available at artists' supply stores and is very inexpensive when purchased in large quantities.

All rice papers are not equally absorbent; the more absorbent papers are best suited to this technique. A sample of paper should be tested before large quantites are purchased.

Two kinds of rice paper were used for the illustrations in this book. Gasenchi Echizen is used to create patterns with sharp lines. Mulberry Student Grade is very absorbent, and is usually moistened with water and squeezed out before it is dipped into the dye, so that the edges of the pattern are softer and more feathery. In addition, Gasenchi Echizen is thinner than Mulberry and and can be folded into smaller shapes.

There are three basic ways to fold the rice paper for dyeing. Each is begun by making accordion pleats along the length of the paper (2-1), forming a long strip that is used for the second step of the folding process.

In 2-2, accordion pleats are made along the length of the folded strip to produce a square or rectangular shape. Illustration 2-3 shows how to make the folds of a right-angle isosceles triangle (half of a square) from 2-1, and 2-4 illustrates how to fold an equilateral triangle. Folds should be made so that all sections of the paper are the same size, and the sections should lie evenly on top of each other when the paper is completely folded. Folded shapes other than those mentioned here may be devised.

Care should be taken not to fold the paper so many times that the folds are not definite. Paper of medium weight, 24 by 33 inches in size, may be folded into about one hundred sections; lightweight paper into more; and heavier paper into fewer. Two or three large sheets may be placed on top of each other and folded together to produce folded patterns with exactly the same design, as long as the folds are not so large that they do not match up neatly.

The food colors employed as dyes are most convenient to use when poured into small, shallow containers such as paint tins or cupcake papers. The colors may be used full strength or diluted with water, and may be blended to any desired hue. Unflavored gelatin may be dissolved in the dye if stiff paper is the desired result.

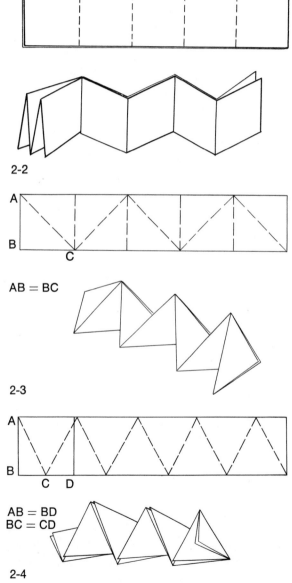

2-2

$AB = BC$

2-3

$AB = BD$
$BC = CD$

2-4

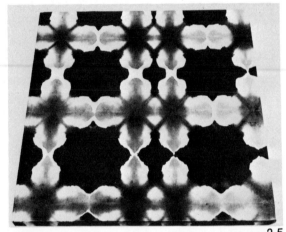

2-5

2-6

2-7

First, the corners or edges of the folded paper are dipped into the dye. Then the folded paper is usually pressed between pieces of cardboard or several layers of newspaper, either by hand or with the foot. This pressure causes the colors to distribute themselves evenly; designs vary according to how much pressure is applied.

The rice paper should then be unfolded to facilitate drying; because the paper is weak when wet, it should be unfolded with great care. The paper may be dried by hanging it on a line or laying it on newspapers. Wet prints should not be allowed to touch one another, lest the colors run. The wet paper may also be stapled carefully to a canvas stretcher to dry (2-5). Paper dried on a canvas stretcher will not be as limp as paper dried on a line, and the creases will be less noticeable.

Creases may be partially pressed out of the finished paper with a warm iron. Care should be taken to prevent water from splashing on the finished paper because food coloring is soluble in water and the pattern will be disturbed if wet again. A clear plastic spray will protect the paper somewhat.

Mulberry rice paper was folded into a square shape and two opposite corners were moistened with water and then squeezed out. To produce 2-6, one corner was dipped into green dye and the diagonally opposite corner into orange, as illustrated in 2-7. Full-strength dyes were used because moistened paper tends to produce a motif of diluted intensity.

2-8

C-2

The Mulberry paper that was used in 2-8 was folded in a square. It was not dipped into water first, and the resulting pattern is sharper than that in 2-6. In 2-9, two opposite corners of the square-folded paper were dipped in color, as in 2-8, but before the paper was unfolded the remaining two corners were dipped in water. The square was held firmly in the center to prevent the water from running too far. The water diluted the colors and left soft, feathery edges contrasting with the remaining sharp edges of the original motif. The same procedure was followed for 2-10, with variations in the resulting design that were unpredictable.

Patterns with a translucent quality are done in two stages. First, a pattern such as the one shown in 2-8 was prepared on Mulberry paper, unfolded, and allowed to dry. When dry, it was refolded, and the two corners that had not previously been colored were dipped briefly in water. The areas into which the water spreads typically appear pale in color, and are outlined in thin lines of intense color (2-11).

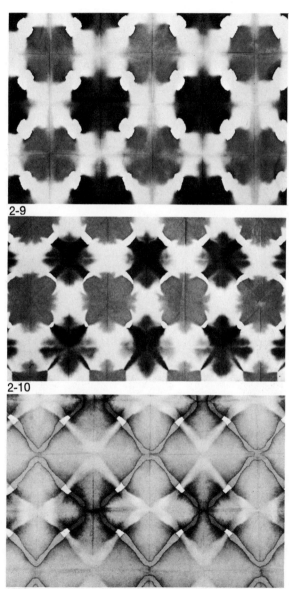

2-9

2-10

2-11

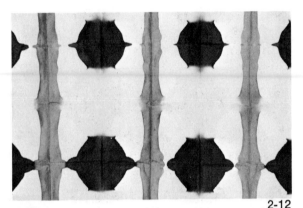

2-12

2-13

2-14

The sharp lines of the motifs in 2-12 were obtained by using Gasenchi Echizen paper. One edge of the square shape was dipped briefly in dye. Then, one of the remaining corners was dipped into another color, and the remaining corner into water. This same paper was used for the pattern in 2-13. The paper was folded into an isosceles triangle (2-14), and each corner was dipped slightly in dye. Note how the motifs at the 45° angles differ from the motifs at the 90° angles. The edges of the paper with a similar design were glued to the inside of an envelope with rubber cement (2-15).

Opposite corners of the folded Mulberry paper were dipped into water and then into dye to produce 2-16. The paper was not squeezed or pressed either before being dipped in the dye or after, and consequently had to be unfolded with great care. The designs in 2-17 and C-3 were obtained using the same method.

In 2-18, the two base angles of an isosceles triangle of Gasenchi Echizen paper were dipped into dye using the special technique of finger pressure: Squeezing the folded paper near the corner between the thumb and forefinger of the right hand (2-19) while dipping the corner into the dye causes the color to run up the folded edges, masking most of the area squeezed between the fingers. The dyed corner is then further squeezed with the thumb and forefinger of the left hand while the right hand keeps its hold; this causes the color to run further up the folded edges. The motifs in the illustration differ according to the amount of pressure used.

2-15

2-17

2-18

2-16

2-19

39

2-20

The finger pressure technique was used only on the smaller motif in 2-20. The corner of Gasenchi Echizen paper folded in a right isosceles triangle was dampened with water and squeezed to make the water run up the folded edges before being dipped into dye. For 2-21, the three angles of an isosceles triangle made of Gasenchi Echizen paper were dampened with water. Then these angles were dyed with the use of finger pressure. The decoration in 2-22 was made from paper of a similar pattern, incorporating three different colors.

The unusual pattern in 2-23 was obtained by refolding a dry sheet of Mulberry paper that had been dyed as in the preceding example, and dipping the shaded parts shown in 2-24 in water, while holding the 90° angle tightly between the thumb and forefinger. The pattern in C-4 was also dyed, dried, refolded, and dipped in water. Designs such as this one are rare, depending on just the right balance of pressure, absorption, and color.

2-21

2-22

2-23

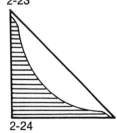

2-24

41

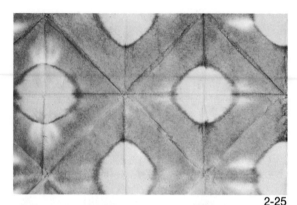

2-25

2-26

2-27

For 2-25, a folded isosceles triangle of Mulberry paper was dampened with water, the right angle dipped in orange dye, and the opposite edge in green. The green dye was permitted to run until it met the orange. The same procedure was used in 2-26 except that the folded paper was not first dipped in water, and the colors were not permitted to run so far. The amount of pressure applied after the dyeing accounts for the sharp edges. The same dyeing method was used in 2-27, except that the right angle was first dipped in water. A similar design was folded into a party hat (2-28) with fringe added. Directions for the party hat, party popper (2-29), and paper bag (2-30) are given in the back of the book.

In 2-31, one of the base angles of an isosceles triangle of Gasenchi Echizen paper was dipped into dye with the application of finger pressure. The opposite edge was dyed another color.

To make 2-32, two corners of a dampened equilateral triangle were dipped into dark dye. Slight irregularities in the folding of the paper account for the variations in the white motif. Dipping two corners of another triangle into dye left a white star shape exposed (2-33). When the paper was dry, it was refolded: the white corner was dipped into water, and then into dye, with the use of finger pressure. When the paper was again dry, the same corner was dipped into water, and then, with the use of finger pressure, into another color dye.

2-28

2-29

2-30

2-31

2-32

2-33

2-34

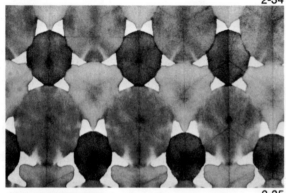

2-35

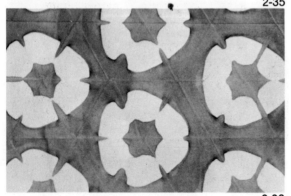

2-36

In 2-34, two corners of an equilateral triangle were dampened, and, with the use of finger pressure, were dipped only slightly in dye. In 2-35, each corner of an equilateral triangle was dipped into a different color dye with application of pressure.

A pattern on either kind of paper can be made by dyeing one corner and the opposite edge of an equilateral triangle (2-36). The resulting circular pattern inspired the paper flowers in 2-37. Directions for making them are given in the back of the book.

It is possible to make small designs on larger sheets of paper if the paper is folded into squares or rectangles instead of triangles. Because Gasenchi Echizen is so thin, it works well for this method. The gift wrapping paper with the smaller design in 2-38 was done in this way, by the method described in 2-9.

To make 2-39, a 6″ × 8″ piece of Gasenchi Echizen paper was folded lengthwise into ⅜″ strips. It was then folded into ⅜″ squares. Held with pliers, as shown in 2-40, three of the corners of the square were dipped into dye. For 2-41, a dry piece of paper that had been previously dyed and rejected as unattractive was folded as in 2-39, and, while held with pliers, was dipped into water. Faint traces of the former pattern can be seen.

The entire paper was immersed in dye, dried, and refolded in 2-42. Three sides were dipped in water. The same procedure was used in 2-43, except that all four sides of the square were dipped in water.

C-3

2-37

2-38

2-39

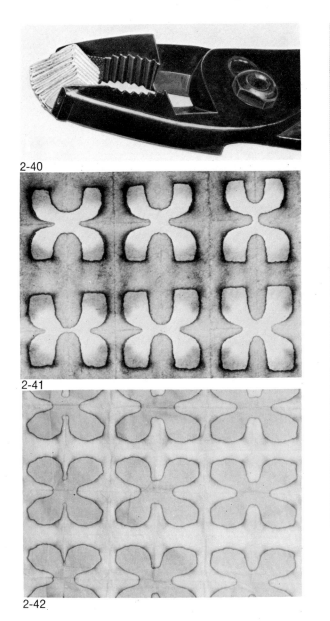

2-40

2-41

2-42

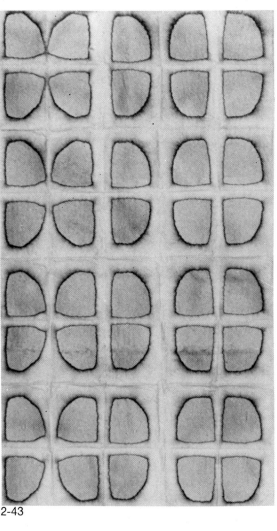

2-43

C-4

For 2-44, a large sheet of Mulberry was folded into a set of squares and dyed as shown in 2-9. When the paper was dry, it was refolded into an isosceles triangle so that the dyed portion would be at the right angle. The two uncolored 45° angles were then dipped slightly in water, and, with the use of finger pressure, were dipped into dye. Another variation of this technique is shown in 2-45.

Sometimes using too much water weakens the color to the extent that the entire design is un-interesting. When this happens, the papers may be refolded and dyed again, although paper so used is less absorbent. Successful designs done in this way depend on experience and skill in handling the dyeing. In 2-46, a washed-out-looking design was dried and then refolded. The corners were dipped slightly in water, and, with the use of finger pressure, were dipped in a strong color.

2-44

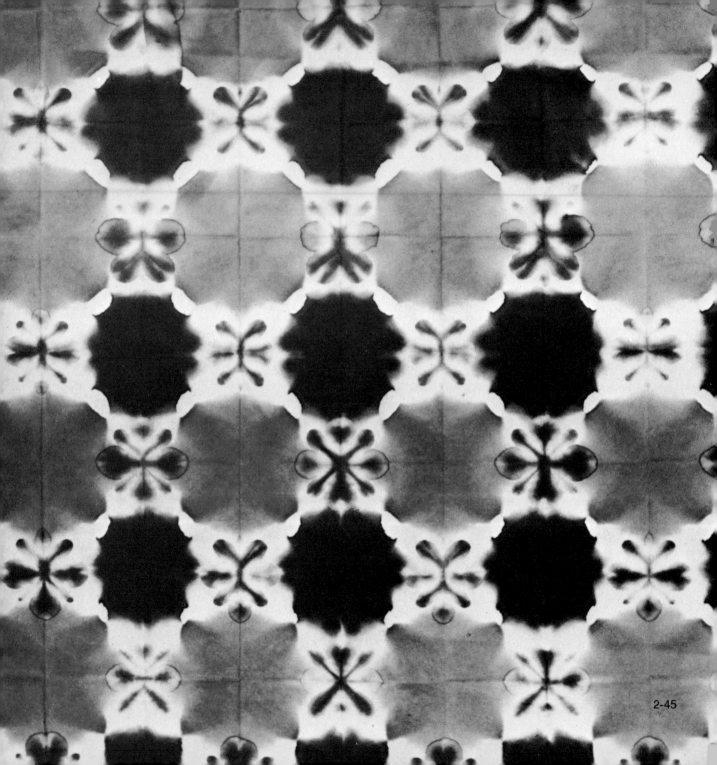

2-45

2-46

2-47

Uneven and irregular folding was responsible for the design made from Gasenchi Echizen paper in 2-47. The fold used to produce the pattern is shown in diagrams 2-48 and 2-49. The right angle of the triangle was dipped in yellow dye (indicated by shading); one of the 45° angles was also dipped in yellow dye, and the dye was allowed to run until the two separate yellow motifs were joined. The remaining 45° angle was dipped in blue (the solid portion of the diagram), with the use of finger pressure.

The example in 2-50 was folded irregularly, too, and the dyeing procedure was like that of 2-36 except that the angle was dyed with the finger-pressure technique.

To make 2-51, a large sheet of Mulberry paper was folded into an equilateral triangle similar to that shown in 2-48 and 2-49. The triangle was dampened slightly, and was held firmly at its approximate center while being dyed. The masking effect of the pressure appears in the finished print as many distorted circles. Illustration 2-5 1 is an irregularly folded equilateral triangle, one corner of which was wet before dyeing.

Other sorts of irregular patterns, like the one in 2-52, may be created by folding paper along lines radiating from a central point (2-53), and then folding the strip obtained into an equilateral triangle.

Illustration 2-54 was folded with no plan and dipped in dye at the corners.

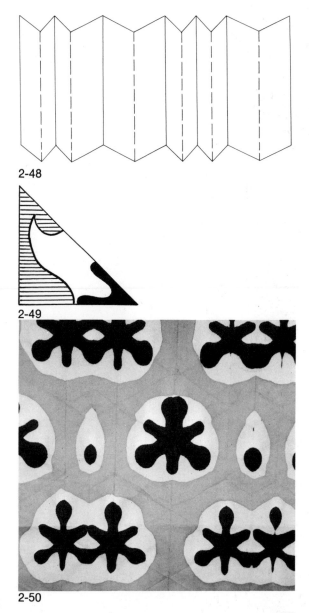

2-48

2-49

2-50

2-51

2-52

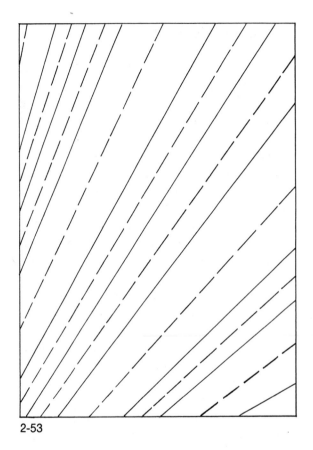

2-53

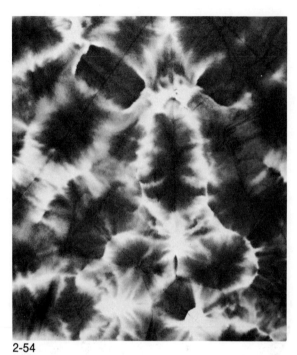

2-54

3. WAX RESIST

3-1

3-2

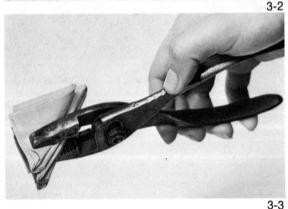

3-3

FOLD & DYE FABRICS

A variation of the fold-and-dye technique for paper may be used to treat fabric, but simply dipping folded fabric into dye does not produce clear motifs. By a method called "wax resist," corners and edges of folded fabric are dipped in wax, forming a mask that prevents the areas it covers from absorbing color when the fabric is immersed in dye. The wax mask makes sharp, clear motifs possible. Such treatment of fabric produces patterns that are negatives of the sort obtained when the fold-and-dye technique is applied to rice paper, since the corners are not touched by color and the rest of the fabric is.

The fabrics best suited to this technique are fine cotton and silk. Heavy materials are too bulky to fold accurately, and drip-dry fabrics do not absorb dye well. Before use, the material should be washed, dried, and ironed. It is advisable to experiment with small squares or retangles of fabric before attempting larger projects.

The fabric is folded along its width into accordion pleats (3-1), which may be held in place with common pins. Ironing the pleats is not necessary, but makes subsequent folds easier. When the material is folded into small squares or triangles (3-2), it is held with a pair of pliers (3-3) to protect fingers from the hot wax. Compression of the fabric with pliers affects the shape of the motif in much the same way that finger pressure affects design when used in fold-and-dye procedures with rice paper.

C-5

3-4

Either paraffin or batik wax may be used as a mask. Because paraffin is brittle, it is likely to crack with handling, permitting dye to bleed into the motifs. In some cases the resulting effect is quite desirable, and is a worthy subject of experimentation. Batik wax, a mixture of paraffin and beeswax, is rather rubbery and does not crack as easily; it is thus more dependable for the beginner. It is available at artists' supply stores.

The wax may be melted in a tin can placed on another tin surface directly over high heat (3-4). The can should be wide enough to accommodate the piece of folded material. Shortly after the wax has melted, the heat should be turned to medium-low. It is advisable to keep a pair of tongs handy for removing the can of wax, should it become necessary. If wax spills on the burner it will catch fire; care should be taken to prevent such accidents. If a safer (though less convenient) method is desired, the wax may be heated in a double boiler and removed from the heat when the folded fabric is to be dipped into it. The pan containing the hot water will keep the wax hot for a while after the double boiler has been removed from the heat.

It is important to keep the wax at the proper temperature. If it is too hot, it will smoke, but it should be at least hot enough to soak through the fabric and penetrate it completely. It is best to test the wax by applying a small amount to the fabric with a small, inexpensive brush kept for this purpose.

After the fabric is waxed, it should be unfolded immediately. It may then be dipped in cold water to thoroughly harden the wax before the fabric is dyed, although this is not always necessary. Because most dyes are dissolved in hot water, the dyebath must be cooled to lukewarm before the waxed fabric is immersed in it, lest the wax be melted by the dye.

Commercial dyes such as Tintex and Rit may be used; they are prepared according to the directions on the package. Batik dyes, available at artists' supply stores, are more brilliant in color than commercial clothing dyes. The fabric should be kept in the dyebath for twenty minutes or more and should be agitated with a stick from time to time to ensure even dyeing. Rubber gloves should be used when removing the fabric from the dye. The dyed fabric is placed between newspapers to absorb excess dye and then hung by the corners to dry. When the fabric is dry, it may be refolded and waxed again; the directions for this procedure are described in some of the examples that follow.

3-5

3-6

When dyeing is completed and the fabric is dry, wax may be removed by either of the following methods. The material may be worked with the fingers to remove thick pieces of wax and then ironed between newspapers. Ironing leaves a stain of wax in the form of an outline around the waxed portions, which sometimes enhances the design. If total removal of the wax is desired, the fabric may be dipped in benzine (this should only be used out-of-doors) or Renuzit (in a well-ventilated room). Care should be taken not to rub the fabric while it is moistened with the cleaning fluid. The material can also be soaked in a pan of very hot water, which melts the wax but also reduces the intensity of the color.

3-7

In 3-5, the material was folded into a right isosceles triangle and the two 45° angles were dipped into batik wax. The pliers were firmly held close to the angle of the folded cloth. The fabric was then unfolded and dyed. In 3-6, the material was folded into a right triangle and dipped in wax at the corners. The triangle was partially unfolded, leaving the accordion pleats undisturbed, and the narrow fabric strip was then refolded into an equilateral triangle, the corners of which were again waxed. The second set of waxed shapes overlapped the waxed shapes made by the right triangle. The material was unfolded and placed in a dyebath, dried, and ironed. Another example of the same technique of superimposed triangles is shown in 3-7. To make 3-8, three corners of an isosceles right triangle were waxed with paraffin instead of batik wax. The dye bled through the cracked areas of the mask. The fabric in 3-9 was dyed with overlapped shapes and paraffin wax was used. In 3-10, the batik-waxed fabric was deliberately squeezed so that the wax would crack. The dark lines are the bleeding of the dye into the waxed areas.

3-8

3-9

3-10

3-11

When fabric is to be dyed in several colors, a separate application of wax is required before each dyeing. The fabric is dyed a light color after the first application of wax. When the fabric is dry, it is refolded lengthwise along the original accordion folds, but the second folding of squares or triangles need not be the same as was used previously. The second set of waxed shapes may overlap the first, but when the fabric is immersed in the dyebath of the second (darker) color, the parts masked before the fabric was immersed in the second bath will remain the color of the first dyebath. The rest of the piece will be dyed by the second color, which will be affected by the color previously used. For example, if the first color used was yellow, the application of blue would change any unmasked yellow areas to a shade of green, but the area masked by the second coating of wax would remain yellow. Examples of this type of waxing and dyeing are shown in 3-11, 3-12, 3-13, and C-12.

In C-5 an equilateral triangle was used. With each successive masking, the corners of the folded fabric were dipped farther into the wax. The fabric was folded into an equilateral triangle in a careless fashion before each application of wax so that outlines of successive triangles did not overlap.

3-12

3-13

3-14

3-15

WIRE SHAPES

Another technique of wax-resist dyeing is to apply wax onto the fabric with a piece of wire, rather than dipping the fabric into wax. The wire is formed into the desired shape, dipped into wax, and then pressed onto the fabric. This creates a wax mask in the same shape as the wire.

A length of wire of medium weight was cut with a pair of pliers and curved into a spiral; enough wire to make a handle was allowed (3-14). The wire was held in the melted wax for a few seconds. When it was lifted out, it was tapped lightly a few times on the inside edges of the can and brought down onto a piece of fabric which had been placed on a piece of cardboard. To ensure that the wire came in contact with the surface of the fabric, a jar top was used to press the top of the wire shape, as shown in 3-15. The wax on the wire penetrated the fabric. The wire must be dipped into wax as described before each application on the fabric. The fabric was then dyed, dried, and ironed between newspapers.

In 3-16, the wire shape shown in 3-14 was stamped so that the second impression was superimposed upside down upon the first. Impressions of the wire shown in 3-17 were arranged in a repeat pattern to make 3-18.

In 3-19, a separate dyebath was used in between the wire maskings so that the colors overlapped.

3-16

Paper rather than fabric may be used with wire masking, except that instead of immersing the paper in the dye after the wax has been applied with the wire shape, the dye is applied to the paper with a soft brush. When dry, the paper is placed between newspaper and the wax is ironed off. In C-6, the wire was first impressed at random on white rice paper, and an orange dye was brushed on. When dry, the paper was again stamped with the same wire in other parts of the rice paper, leaving the original wax on, and brushed with black dye. When dry, the paper was placed between newspaper and the wax was ironed off.

Illustration 3-20 is a combination of fold-and-dye technique with both wire stamping and the application of a wax mask with a brush. A paper that had already been folded and dyed was waxed with a brush in some areas and stamped with waxed wire in others. The paper was then brushed with black dye, as in C-6.

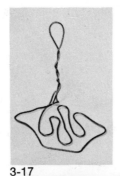

3-17

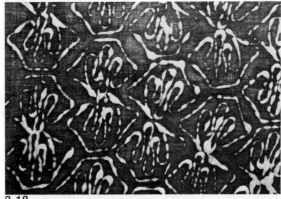

3-18

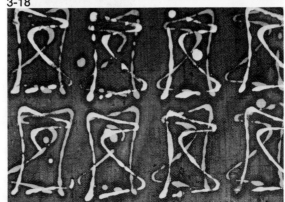

3-19

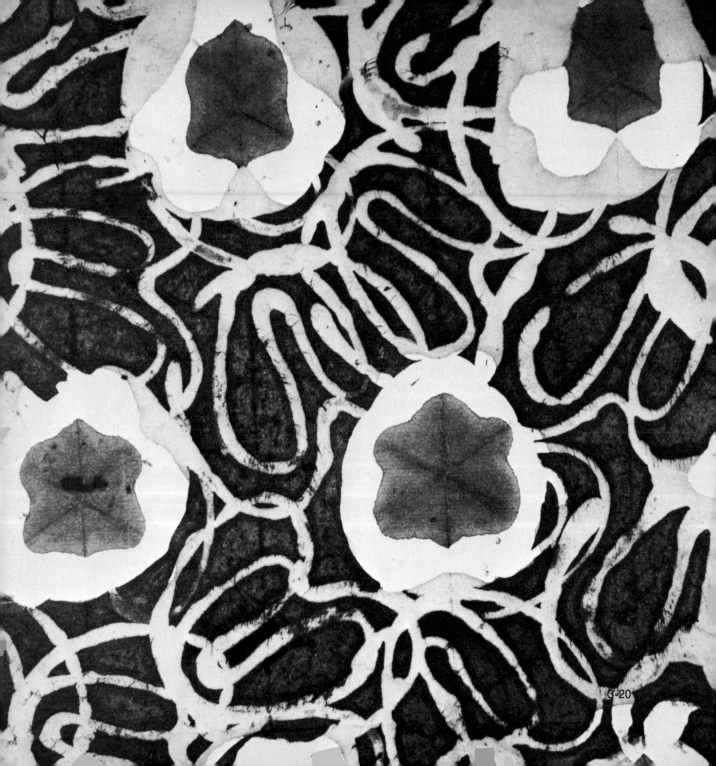

3-20

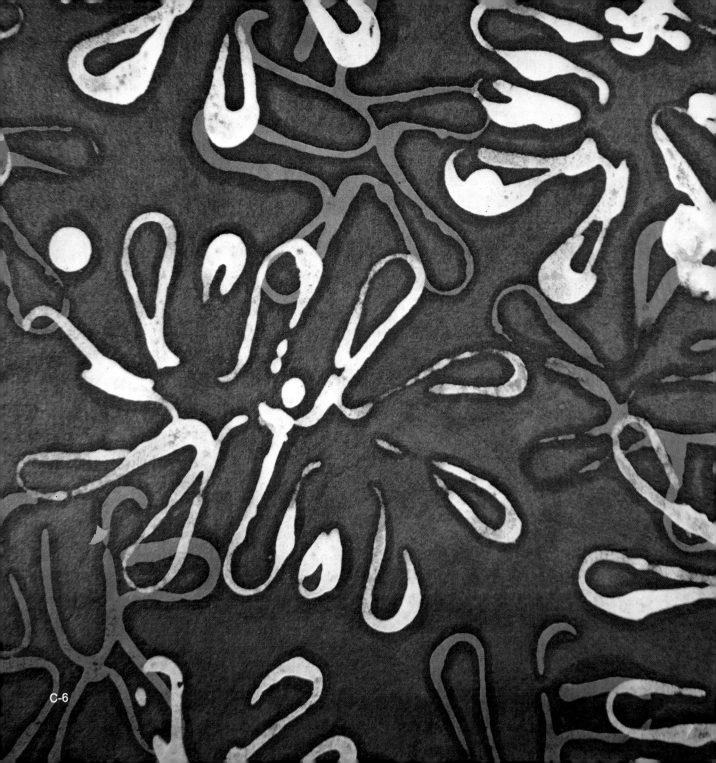

C-6

4. SEWING MACHINE STITCHERY

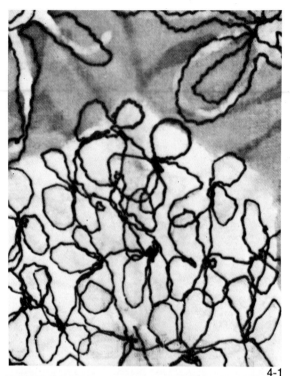

4-1

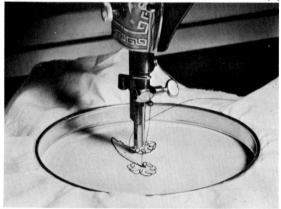

4-2

The stitch of a sewing machine may be used to accent the shapes on dyed fabrics or papers, as in example 4-1, by making a few changes in normal procedure for operating an electric sewing machine. The presser foot is removed, and the material to be stitched is placed in a hoop. The hoop is placed under the needle, and the presser foot lever is lowered (4-2). When the motor is started, the hoop can be maneuvered with the hands in any direction.

Before the first application of dye to 4-1, shown in color in C-7, the large areas were masked with wax as in the fold-and-dye technique, and other areas of the fabric were covered with wax impressions of a wire stamp. After the dye had dried, more wax impressions were made with the same stamp, and the fabric was immersed in the second color of dye. When the wax had been removed from the fabric, black thread was used to accent the various shapes.

In 4-3 and 4-4, bits of scraps of material from wax-resist patterns on fabric were cut out and appliquéd onto burlap using the hoop and the sewing machine stitch. In 4-5, a section of fold-and-dye paper was outlined in machine stitchery. In 4-6, parts of a fold-and-dye paper pattern were cut out and appliquéd to cloth.

C-7

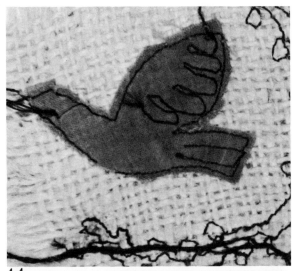

4-4

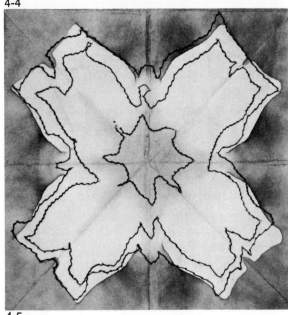

4-5

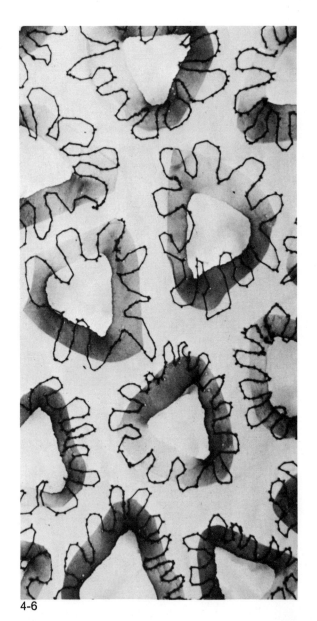

4-6

71

5. POTATO PRINTING

5-1

5-2

5-3

Printing repeated patterns on paper with a block into which a design has been carved is a technique commonly employed in graphics. One of the simplest printing tools is the potato, which is easily carved and insignificant in cost. Consequently, one may indulge in experimenting with spontaneous and unusual carvings, which may produce quite interesting and unexpected results.

A piece of glass may be used for a palette, but waxed paper taped to cardboard is equally suitable. A thin layer of ink is spread on the palette with a paint spatula and is replaced as it dries or is used up.

Either block-printing ink or acrylic paint may be used for printing. Acrylic paint dries quickly on the palette and is not water soluble when dry. Block-printing ink remains moist on the palette, but it is soluble in water. Therefore, papers that have been printed with block-printing ink might be treated with a fixative such as plastic spray, to protect the design.

The potato block is made by cutting the potato crosswise with a paring knife. Cutting the potato with a sawing motion usually produces the flat surface required for successful printing. The block is then cut so that the printing surface is a basic shape such as a square, rectangle, or triangle (5-1), and small pieces of potato are cut or gouged from this surface to form the motif. Printing is done by dipping the potato block into the ink on the palette and then applying it to the paper.

The block for the pattern in 5-2 was made by cutting four wedges from the potato with a paring knife (5-3). The design was printed repeatedly, producing a negative pattern of diamonds. Uneven distribution of the ink, characteristic of potato prints, lends charm to the design.

A linoleum-cutting tool (5-4), fitted with a V-shaped gouge, may be used to carve thin lines in the potato block. The gouge was used to remove pieces from the block shown in 5-5. In the printed pattern of 5-6, the lines that were gouged out add a new element to the negative design. A diamond shape cut from a potato was used to print alternate red and black diamonds in the pattern in C-8.

Triangular wedges were cut from opposite edges of a square block and grooves were gouged from the remaining portion of the block's surface in 5-7. The grooves adjacent to the triangles are wide, so that white X-shaped motifs appear in the negative of the finished print. Variation in the intensity of the motifs was achieved by making several impressions with the printing block between applications of ink, so that the ink became progressively paler.

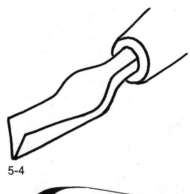

5-4

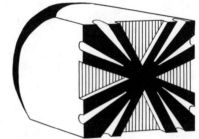

5-5

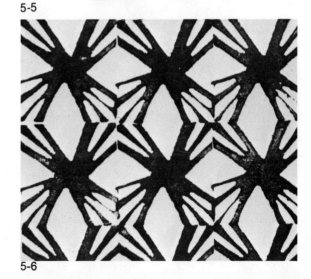

5-6

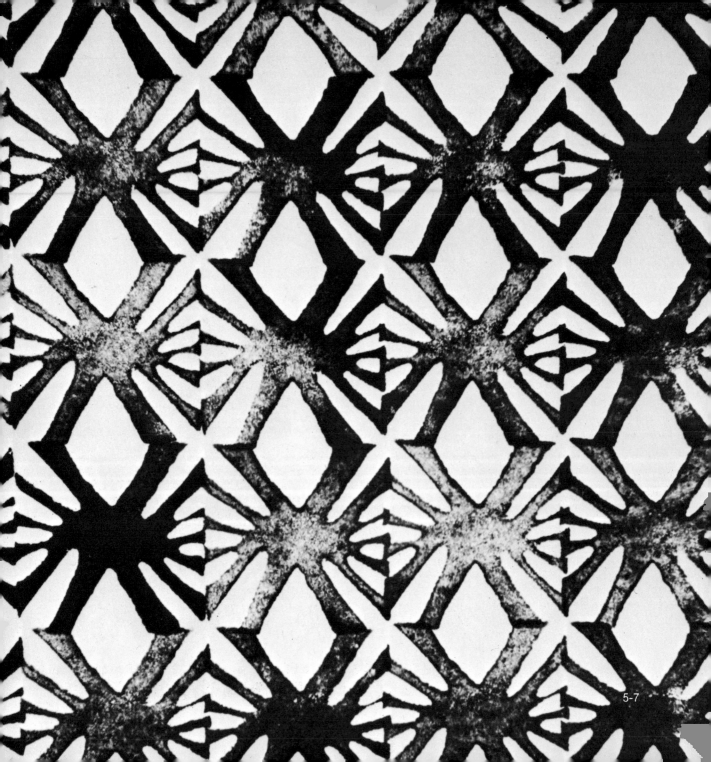

5-7

The block used to make the print that covers a note pad in 5-8 was made by cutting wedges from a square potato block. Directions for making the pad cover are given in the back of the book.

In 5-9, grooves were cut spontaneously in a square block with a linoleum-cutting gouge.

In 5-10, a square block was cut with diagonal grooves. No attempt was made to cut the block so that the lines would meet in the resulting design (5-11). The block was turned with each successive printing.

A U-shaped gouge on a linoleum-cutting tool (5-12) was used to make the central circle in the motif shown in 5-13. The curved lines were made by carving away surrounding areas with repeated use of the V-shaped gouge. It was intended that the lines vary in thickness. When the motif was repeated, an unexpected negative design emerged (5-14).

The grooves cut in a rectangular block (5-15) were not quite parallel, and some did not cut completely across the block. The block was turned at each printing in 5-16, leaving a negative pattern of white squares.

5-8

5-9

5-10

5-11

5-12

5-13

5-14

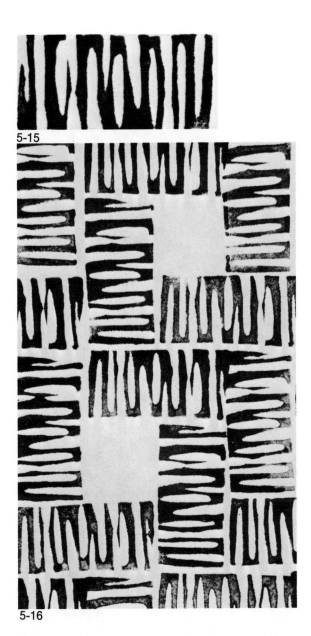

5-15

5-16

77

5-17

5-19

5-18

5-20

Sometimes a simple, spontaneous carving develops into a more complicated motif. A U-shaped gouge was used to remove pieces from diagonally opposite corners of a square block of potato (5-17). A test print (5-18) revealed the suggestion of a floral motif. The block was refined by removing the dark areas so that only outlines of the design remained (5-19). The result, 5-20, was a pattern of diamonds and blossoms. In 5-21, the same block was printed without changing directions.

Three spontaneously curved gouges inspired a refined leaf pattern, shown in 5-22. The leaf motif was printed so that the triangle in the upper right corner of the block joined the leaf in the upper left corner, forming a long leaf, and lending continuity to the finished pattern (5-23).

Spontaneous use of the U-shaped gouge was employed in carving a variety of shapes from a rectangular potato block (5-24). Repeated impressions of the block produced an unexpected pattern reminiscent of antique wallpaper (5-25).

The design in C-9 was adapted from a fragment of a contemporary paper printed in Western Germany. Its charm lies in its spontaneous and childlike quality, its graceful shapes, and the delightful use of superimposed printing.

5-21

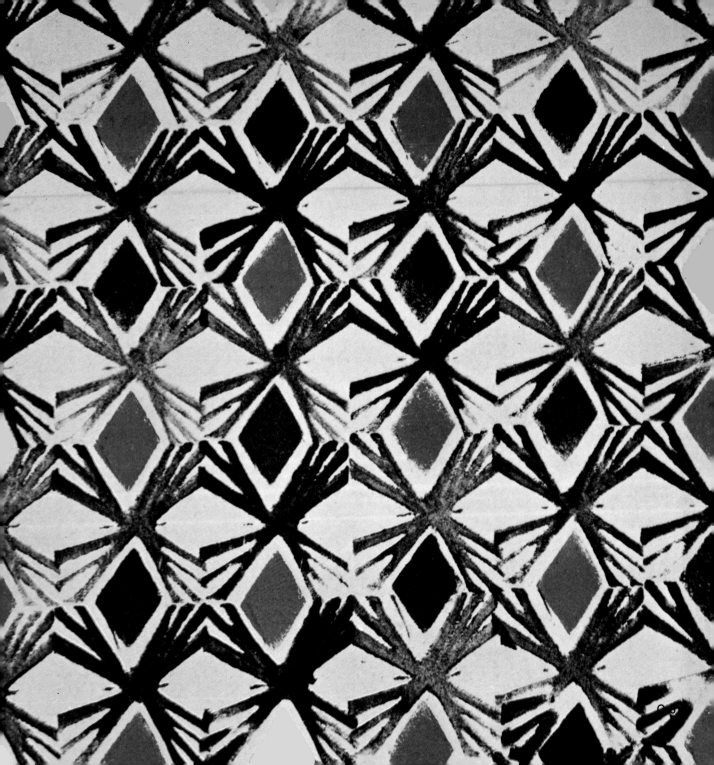

5-22

5-23

C-9

5-24

5-25

6. STARCH PAPERS

6-1

Ink may be replaced as a printing medium with a mixture of cornstarch and paint called starch paint. Starch papers, as the resulting prints are sometimes called, were first used by early bookbinders for covering books, but were later replaced with machine-printed papers. No special skill is needed to work with starch paint, although experience enables one to have greater control over the results.

Starch paint is made as follows: Two tablespoons of cornstarch are mixed with two tablespoons of cold water in a saucepan. One cup of boiling water is added, and the mixture is brought to a boil, while being stirred. When the mixture is cool, it can be poured into several small containers, and color added to each, to make the desired shades. Either powdered batik dyes or acrylic paint may be used; the batik dyes give a particularly brilliant color.

The wet mixture is brushed on paper and an impression is made by pressing a hard object—such as a potato, a cardboard comb, or a linoleum cut—into the paint. This pressure displaces the paint, and a veined pattern is left by the object as it picks up part of the mixture when lifted from the paper. The veins and the thin ridge of paint formed along the edges of the pattern are raised when wet but, when dry, become flush with the surface of the paper and dry as dark outlines. The colors are permanent; a fixative will give them a smoother surface. One advantage of this technique is that if a mistake is made the paper may be brushed with more paint and redesigned, as is done in finger painting.

In 6-1, an inexpensive paint brush, about an inch wide, was used to apply starch paint to a piece of paper, and a potato block was impressed in the paint. When using a cut potato block to make impressions in the starch paint, it is best to twist the block very slightly, to displace the paint as much as possible. Areas in contact with the surface of the potato have the veined appearance characteristic of this technique. After each impression, the paint on the potato was used to make another print on plain white paper. Thus, two decorative papers are obtained, one a negative of the other. In 6-2, a print was made by sliding the potato block downward a distance of a half-inch as each impression was made. In 6-3, the potato block was twisted 45 degrees as it was impressed on the painted paper.

The light-colored design in 6-4 was carved from a potato and printed on a textured paper.

6-2

6-3

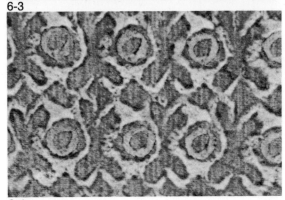

6-4

6-5

6-6

A wood-grain effect was obtained in 6-5 by brushing several related colors of starch next to each other. In some places the brush was pushed in the opposite direction to that of its usual stroke (6-6), so that on the upward strokes the bristles spread outward and displaced the paint brushed on with the downward strokes.

A cardboard comb, made by cutting V-shaped wedges from the edge of a piece of cardboard, may be used to trace lines in starch paint (6-7). The teeth of the comb should be parallel to the grain of the cardboard, in order that it be relatively inflexible. The direction of the grain is perpendicular to the lines along which the cardboard bends most easily, as illustrated in 6-8. A comb was used to draw curved lines through rows of multicolored starch-painted paper. The paper was used to cover a one-signature book (6-9), directions for which are given in the back of the book.

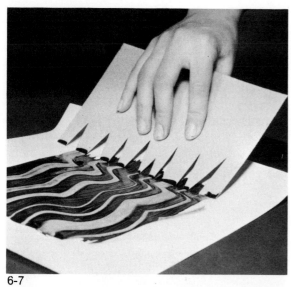

6-7

6-9

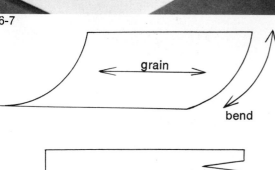

grain

bend

6-8

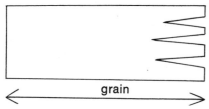

grain

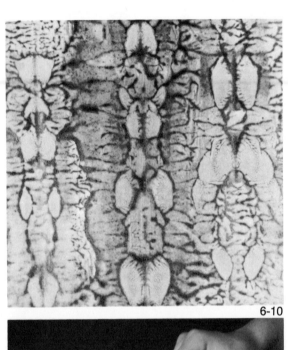

6-10

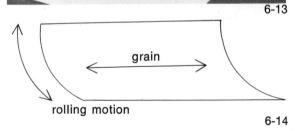

6-12

6-13

6-11

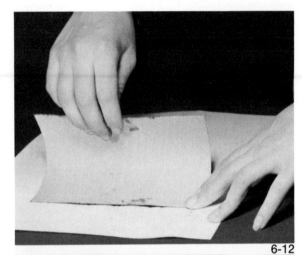

grain

rolling motion

6-14

88

The paper shown in 6-10 was covered with starch paint and folded lightly, but not allowed to touch except where pressed with the fingers, so that mirror images were formed on either side of the fold (6-11). In this case the fingers act as the object that makes the impression on the paper.

Starch prints depicting trees or shrubs may be made with a different technique. A variety of colors are brushed onto a sheet of thin cardboard. The cardboard is laid onto the surface of a sheet of paper with a rolling motion, starting at the top of the cardboard and lifted off at the bottom (6-12 and 6-13). Because this manner of printing requires the cardboard to be flexible, the cardboard must be held so that the grain is perpendicular to the direction of the rolling motion (6-14). The resulting print (6-15) has the appearance of a wooded area.

A piece of cardboard about 2 by 4 inches was used to repeat the pattern in 6-16. A linoleum cut of a rabbit (6-17) was dipped in starch paint and then printed in the corner of a starch print, made by the cardboard technique, that looks like a wintertime scene of a field. Starch prints of this type also make appropriate backgrounds for silhouettes, illustrations, or dioramas.

Paper can be brushed with water in some places before being impressed with the rolling cardboard. The water causes the color to blend, producing a contrast in texture (6-18, 6-19, and 6-20).

6-15

6-16

6-17

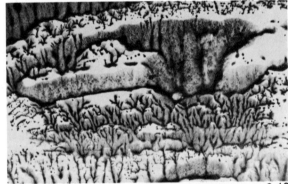

6-18

6-19

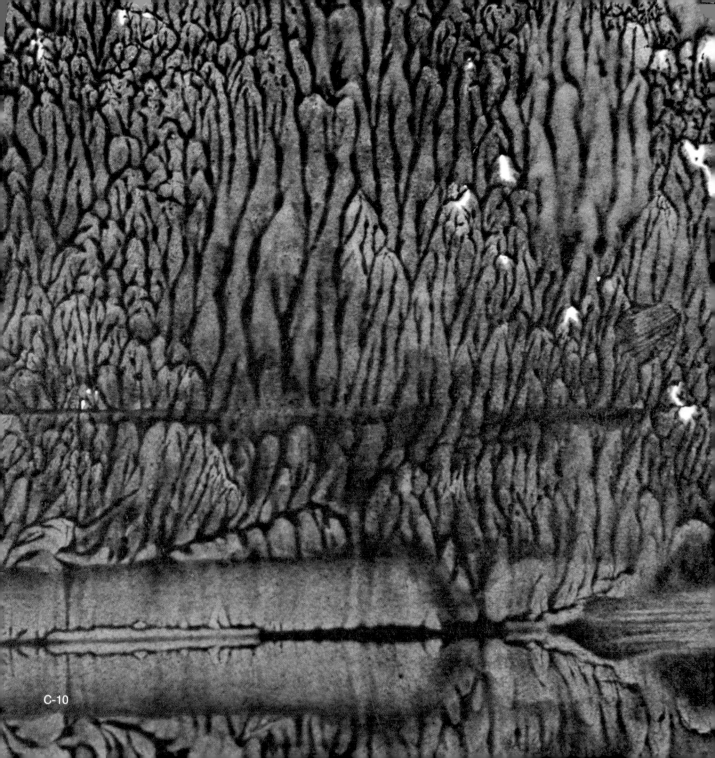

C-10

6-20

6-21

Starch paint was brushed on paper rather than on the cardboard; then clean cardboard was rolled over the painted paper. As the cardboard pulled away, it left veined patterns of paint on the paper (6-21).

In C-10, a forest print was made with cardboard and then folded. The mirror image under the fold makes the print look like a lake reflecting a forest.

Although some control may be used to get patterns such as the one in 6-22, in general the final effect is accidental.

There are many possible variations of this technique, and, as one works, other ways of applying paint with cardboard suggest themselves. For example, the cardboard may be brushed with one color paint and rolled onto another color that has been applied to the paper. Rows of colors may be brushed on a glass palette, picked up with the cardboard, and transferred to the paper.

C-11 is a collage of sections of fold-and-dye paper, origami paper, and colored tissue paper. An uncolored cornstarch mixture was brushed on a large sheet of paper, and the colored papers, torn into various shapes, were arranged on the clear starch, to which they easily adhered. More uncolored starch was applied over the papers; care was taken to prevent the colors from running. When the starch was dry, cardboard was brushed with black starch paint and rolled onto the collage, as in the previous illustrations, but with a lighter touch, to transfer a black starch print over the collage.

6-22

C-11

DIRECTIONS FOR MAKING PROJECTS

COVER FOR MARBLED PAD

(illustrated in 1-32)

Figure 1: Cut mat board (¹⁄₁₆″ thick) with a #11 mat-knife blade in a mat-knife holder, or a paper cutter. Cut with the grain running parallel to the length of the spine A (see 6-8). B is the top cover of the pad, and C is the bottom cover. The top of the pad in this example is next to the spine and is indicated by crosshatching. B and C are cut so that the pad is almost flush with the side next to spine A, and with a ⅛″ allowance on each of the other three sides. Spine A is the width of the thickness of the pad and the length of B and C.

Figure 2: Arrange A, B, and C on a piece of solid-colored bookcloth, allowing about ³⁄₃₂″ between A and B, and A and C. Cut the bookcloth ⅝″ wider on each of the four sides. Place the book-cloth right side down on newspaper. Using a ½″ bristle brush, spread the wrong side with white glue that has been thinned with water, brushing from the center outward. Discard the newspaper. Place the spine in the center. Before the glue dries, quickly add boards B and C, allowing ³⁄₃₂″ between the spine and the boards.

Figure 3: With scissors, miter the corners ⅛″ from the corner of the board.

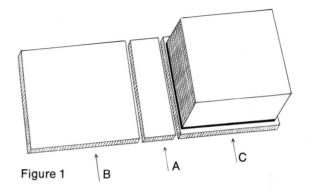

Figure 1

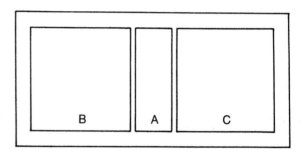

Figure 2

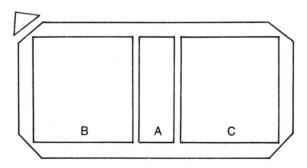

Figure 3

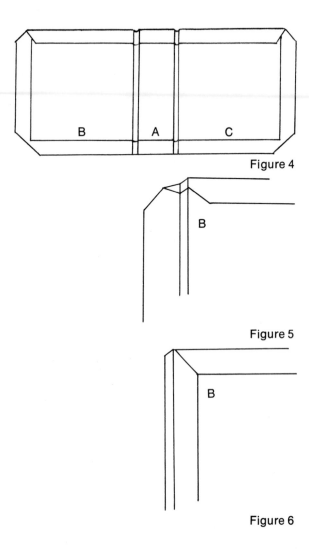

Figure 4

Figure 5

Figure 6

Figure 4: Replace glue where needed and fold the top of the cloth down onto the boards, making sure it fits tightly next to the edge of the board. Use a tongue depressor or bookbinder's bone folder to press between A, B, and C, and make contact between the bookcloth and the board. Place clean white paper between the bone or tongue depressor and the cloth when rubbing, to avoid leaving a shine on the bookcloth. Turn up the bottom in the same way.

Figure 5: Before turning in the sides, indent all four of the corners with a fingernail or bone folder.

Figure 6: Turn the sides onto the board. Bone down.

Figure 7: The lining for the inside of the spine is cut of bookcloth. It is the length of the spine of the pad and the width of the thickness of the pad plus 1″. Place the cloth right side down on a piece of newspaper and glue the wrong side of the cloth. Discard the newspaper. Place the lining on the spine, using a bone folder to rub the cloth onto the spine, into the crevices between A and B, B and C, and then onto B and C.

Figure 8: Cut a piece of heavy-grade white drawing paper the size of the pad and glue it to the center of B. Glue the pad to C, keeping the top almost flush with the edge of C and allowing equal space on the other three edges. Place a piece of waxed paper between the pad and the front cover B, close the cover, and keep under the weight of several books overnight. When using fabric instead of bookcloth, the glue should be applied to the mat board instead of directly on the fabric. Otherwise the procedure is the same.

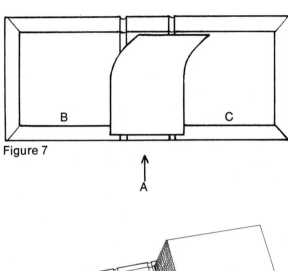

Figure 7

B   C

A

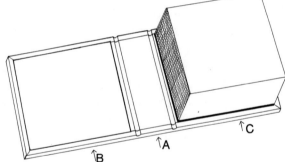

Figure 8

B   A   C

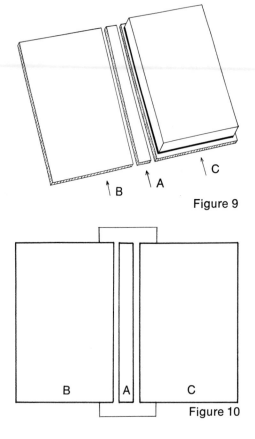

Figure 9

Figure 10

NOTE-PAD COVER

(illustrated in 5-8)

Figure 9: Following the directions given in Figure 1, cut the mat board to the dimensions of a 3″ × 5″ pad. The top of the pad in this example is at the top of C.

Figure 10: Cut a strip of 1½″-wide Mystik tape of an appropriate color 1″ longer than A. Center A on the Mystik tape and place B and C on each side, allowing $\frac{1}{16}$″ between A and B, and A and C. Since Mystik tape is self-adhering, no glue is needed.

Figure 11: Fold the Mystik tape down onto the boards A, B, and C, and press into the crevices between the boards.

Figure 12: Fold the Mystik tape up onto the boards at the bottom. Cut another length of Mystik tape exactly the length of the pad and apply to the spine of the inside of the cover.

Figure 13: Cut the decorative paper so that it will overlap the long edge of the tape $\frac{1}{16}$″. The three remaining sides are cut $\frac{5}{8}$″ wider on each side. Place the decorative paper right side down on newspaper and spread from the center outward with diluted glue. Discard the newspaper. Close the cover as shown in the diagram, and place it horizontally in front of you. This enables you to apply the decorative paper so that it is parallel to the edge of the spine. Pick up the decorative paper by the edges and place $\frac{1}{16}$″ over the Mystik tape. Bone to smooth out wrinkles, using clean white paper between the decorative paper and the bone to prevent the paper from tearing.

Figure 14: Miter the corners as in Figure 3 and fold the overlap down onto the board as in Figure 4.

Figure 15: Indent the corners as in Figure 5 and fold the overlap onto the board as in Figure 6. Repeat the steps in Figures 13, 14, and 15 on the other side of the cover.

Figure 16: To make a pocket for the pad so that it can be replaced when used up, wrap a piece of paper around the thin cardboard back (indicated by the heavy black line in the diagram) to which the pad is attached. The paper should be slightly shorter than the pad and should overlap the width of the pad by ½″. Glue the edge of E to the edge of D. Then apply glue to the entire surface between the dotted lines.

Figure 17: With the pad still in the pocket, place the glued pocket onto C close to the spine, allowing an equal margin on the other three sides. Cut heavy-grade white paper the size of the pad and glue to the center of B. Place waxed paper between the pad and front cover and keep under weight overnight. Bookcloth or fabric may be used instead of Mystik tape; with these, glue must of course be used.

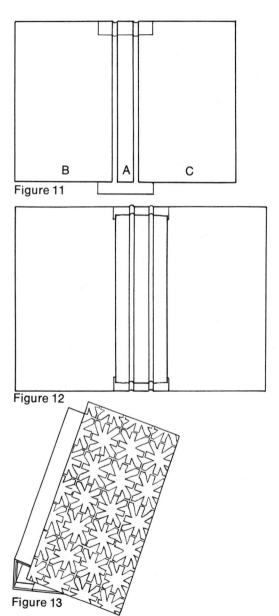

B   A   C

Figure 11

Figure 12

Figure 13

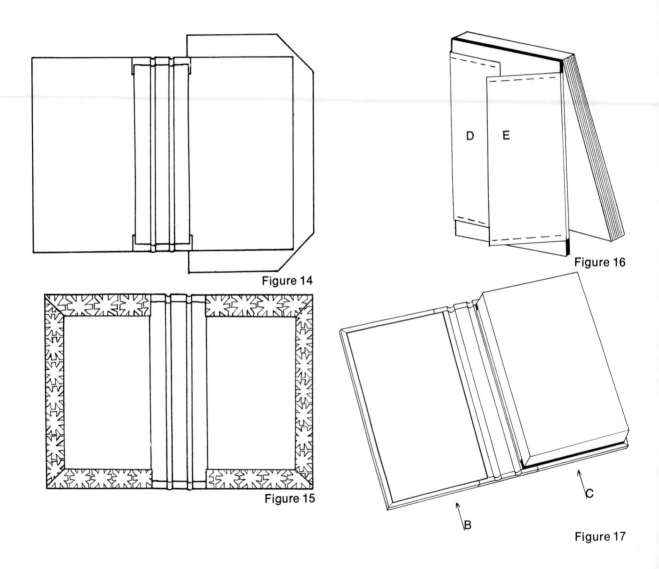

Figure 14

Figure 16

Figure 15

Figure 17

PAPER BAG

(illustrated in 2-30)

Figure 18: Place a 12″ × 20″ sheet of decorated paper wrong side up, and fold down 1″ along the longer measurement to make a hem, as shown by the dotted line on the right of the diagram. This forms the top of the bag. Overlap the paper ½″ along the shorter measurement, tucking one edge of the hem into the other, and glue together the overlapped edges. Arrange the hem neatly and glue down. Fold in the sides of the bag as shown.

Figure 19: Flatten the folded paper. The measurement from the bottom of the bag (C) to the dotted line (D) should be greater than the distance from A to B in Figure 18 by at least ½″. Since the distance from A to B in this example is 3″, the dotted line is drawn 3½″ from the end.

Figure 20: Fold the paper upward along the dotted line.

Figure 21: Spread out E and F with the thumbs and index fingers, placing the thumbs on the inside and pushing down. This will form a triangle like the one at G. Crease along the base of the triangle. Repeat on the other side.

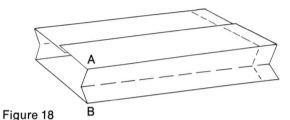

Figure 18

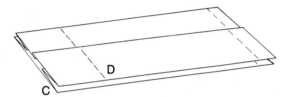

Figure 19

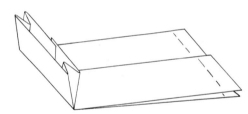

Figure 20

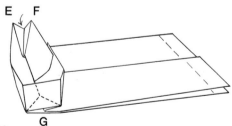

Figure 21

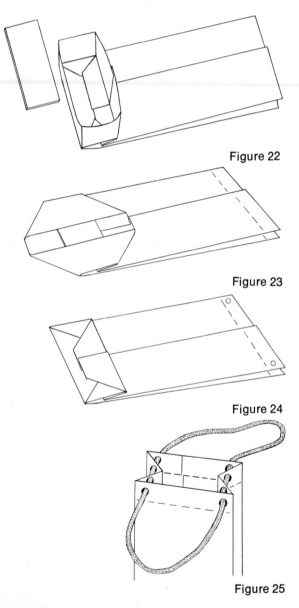

Figure 22

Figure 23

Figure 24

Figure 25

Figure 22: Crease along the long edges between the corners of the triangles, to form the bottom of the bag. Cut a piece of thin cardboard the exact size of the bottom.

Figure 23: Fold down the two sides and glue to the cardboard base.

Figure 24: Fold down the remaining two sides and glue one onto the other. With a paper puncher, punch holes through all thicknesses at the circles indicated at the top of the bag.

Figure 25: Run a cord through the holes. Open the bag and tie the knot on the inside of the bag so that it cannot be seen. This type of bag can be made in any size square or rectangle and in any length, following the above principles.

C-12

PAPER HAT

(illustrated in 2-28)

Figure 26: Fold a 12″ × 16″ sheet of decorated paper in half.

Figure 27: Dotted line B-E marks the center of the folded sheet of paper.

Figure 28: Bring A-B to B-E and C-B to B-E.

Figure 29: Fold D-F upward along the line made by A and C. Repeat on other side.

Figure 30: Lay several sheets of decorated paper on top of each other and cut through them with scissors as shown in the diagram.

Figure 31: Roll up the cut paper as shown and spread apart the fringe. Staple to the top of the hat.

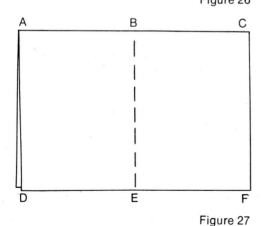

Figure 26

Figure 27

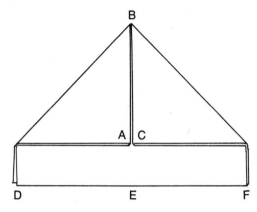

Figure 28

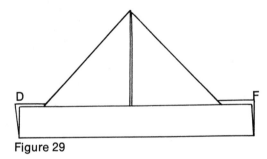

Figure 29

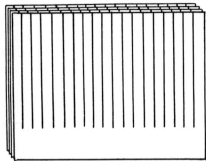

Figure 30

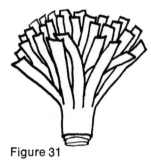

Figure 31

PARTY POPPER

(illustrated in 2-29)

Figure 32: Cut a thin piece of cardboard 2½″ × 3¼″ with the grain running as indicated by the arrow (*see* 6-8).

Figure 33: Roll the cardboard into a cylinder and tape the ends together.

Figure 34: Take a piece of 6″ × 10″ decorated rice paper. Cut strips 4″ in length from each side, as shown in the diagram. (In order to save time in cutting, the paper may be folded in quarters and cut.)

Figure 35: Wrap the rice paper around the cardboard cylinder (which has first been filled with goodies) and tie at each end. (The diagram shows one end tied.)

Figure 32

Figure 33

Figure 34

Figure 35

HANGING DECORATION

(illustrated in 2-22)

Figure 36: Accordion-fold a piece of decorative paper approximately three times longer than it is wide. The example shown in 2-22 is made from a piece of paper 9″ × 26″, and the pleats are 1″ wide.

Figure 37: Staple the pleats together at the center, fan out the edges, and bring down A to meet B and C to meet D. Staple the ends together. Hang from a string fastened to one of the staples.

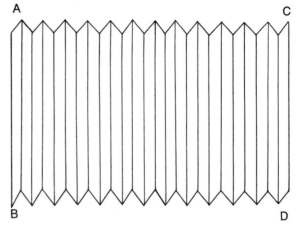

Figure 36

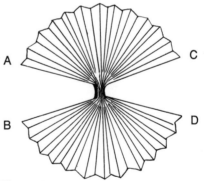

Figure 37

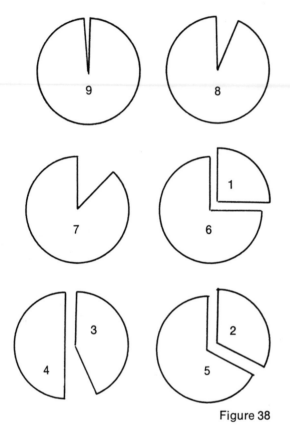

Figure 38

PAPER FLOWERS

(illustrated in 2-37)

Figure 38: Cut six circles out of paper decorated with the design in 2-36. The circles in the diagram indicate the way to cut the shapes of the petals, and are numbered accordingly from the smallest to the largest.

Figure 39: Use white glue to join the two open ends together to form a cone from each of the nine pieces. Snip the apex of each cone, as shown by the dotted line in the diagram.

Figure 40: Curl one end of a piece of covered floral wire and string the nine cones on the other end, starting with the smallest and ending with the largest.

Figure 41: Push all the petals together and make a figure eight with the wire, close to the outside of the largest petal.

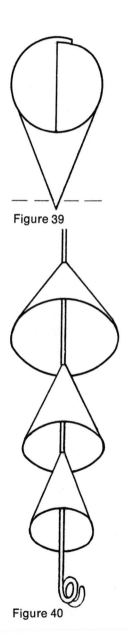

Figure 39

Figure 40

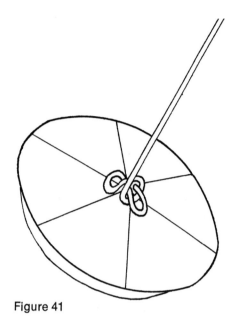

Figure 41

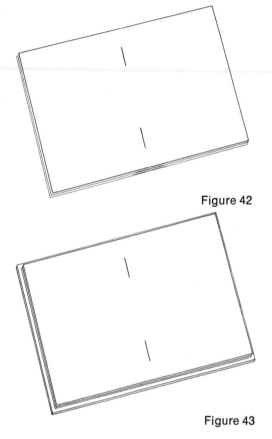

Figure 42

Figure 43

SINGLE-SIGNATURE BOOKLET

(illustrated in 6-9)

Figure 42: Stack six to ten sheets of 4″ × 6″ paper and staple or sew them together in the center, leaving ⅝″ from the staple or stitch to the edge of the page.

Figure 43: Cut a piece of thin cardboard ⅛″ larger than the paper on each side. The cardboard will measure 4¼″ × 6¼″ for this example.

Figure 44: Using the cardboard as a template, cut a piece of decorative paper ⅝″ wider than the cardboard on each side.

Figure 45: Fold the extra ⅝″ over the cardboard on each of the four sides to make creases. Set aside the cardboard.

Figure 46: Miter the corners of the decorated paper at the four points where the folds intersect. Place the booklet on the center of the inside of the decorative paper. Bring the folded edge of the decorative paper over only the bottom sheet of the booklet on all four sides. Close the book and press the folded (sewn) center edge firmly.

Figure 47: Open the book. Apply glue to the area on the bottom sheet of the booklet that is shown crosshatched in the diagram. Repeat on the other side of the book. Close the book and place under pressure.

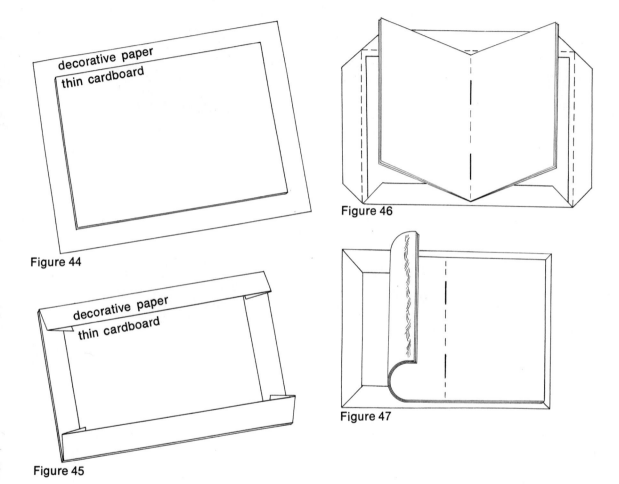

decorative paper
thin cardboard

Figure 44

decorative paper
thin cardboard

Figure 45

Figure 46

Figure 47

111

SOURCES OF SUPPLIES

SUPPLIES

(numbers refer to sources listed)
acrylic paint   2, 3
batik dyes and batik wax   2, 3
bone folders   4, 7, 9, 10
bookcloth   4, 5, 7, 9, 10
embroidery hoop   11
food coloring   5, 8
linoleum-cutting tools   2, 3
marbling moss   5, 7, 9, 10
mat board   2, 3
oil-base inks   2, 3
paraffin wax   8, 11
rice papers   1, 2, 3
rubber cement   2, 3, 11
tongue depressors   6
white glue   2, 3, 11

SOURCES

1   Andrews/Nelson/Whitehead, 7 Laight Street, New York, N.Y. 10013
2   Artists' supply stores
3   Arthur Brown & Bro., Inc., 2 West 46 Street, New York, N.Y. 10036
4   Basic Crafts Co., 312 East 23 Street, New York, N.Y. 10010
5   Bookcraft, Box 6048, Hamden, Conn. 06517
6   Drug stores
7   Dryad Ltd., Northgates, Leicester, England
8   Grocery stores
9   Russell Bookcrafts, Hitchin, England
10   Talas, 104 Fifth Ave., New York, N.Y. 10011
11   Variety stores

FURTHER READING

Bystrom, Ellen. PRINTING ON FABRICS. New York: Van Nostrand Reinhold Company, 1971. *Basic techniques of fabric decoration.*

Cockerell, Sydney M. MARBLING AS A SCHOOL SUBJECT (pamphlet). Russell Bookcrafts. (See Supply Source #9)

COMBED PATTERN PAPERS (pamphlet). Leicester: The Dryad Press. (See Supply Source #4, 7)

"Cover A Book To Look Like A Million," WOMAN'S DAY MAGAZINE, February, 1970. (Available from Fawcett Publications, Inc., New York) *Colored photographs of various bookcover designs by Annette Hollander.*

COVER A BOOK TO LOOK LIKE A MILLION (pamphlet). New York: Fawcett Publications, Inc., 1970. (See Supply Source #5). *Detailed instructions by Annette Hollander for making bookcovers and decorated papers.*

"Fold Dye Papers," WOMAN'S DAY MAGAZINE, September, 1970. *Colored photographs and detailed instructions for fold-and-dye papers designed by Annette Hollander.*

Hasluck, Paul N. BOOKBINDING. London: Cassell and Company Ltd., c. 1900. *Chapter on other methods of marbling.*

Hewitt-Bates, J. S. BOOKBINDING. 7th ed. Leicester: The Dryad Press, 1962. *Chapters on the graining of paper and another method of marbling.*

Hewitt-Bates, J. S., and Halliday, J. THREE METHODS OF MARBLING (pamphlet). Leicester: The Dryad Press. (See Supply Source #8)

Johnson, Pauline. CREATING WITH PAPER. Seattle: University of Washington Press, 1958. *Ideas for using decorative papers.*

————. CREATIVE BOOKBINDING. Seattle: University of Washington Press, 1963. *Extensive chapter on decorated papers.*

Lauterburg, Lotti. FABRIC PRINTING. New York: Reinhold Publishing Corporation, 1963. *Other methods of printing on fabric.*

Loring, Rosamond B. DECORATED BOOK PAPERS. Cambridge: Harvard University Press, 1952. *Chapters on other methods of marbling and paste papers.*

O'Brien, James. DESIGN BY ACCIDENT. New York: Dover Publications, Inc., 1968.

Town, Laurence. BOOKBINDING BY HAND. London: Faber and Faber, c. 1950. *Chapter on a different method of marbling.*

Yamada, Sadami, and Ito, Kiyotada. NEW DI-
MENSIONS IN PAPER CRAFT. Rev. ed. New
York: Japan Publications Trading Company,
1967. *Ideas for using decorative papers.*

"Your Own Decorative Papers," WOMAN'S DAY
MAGAZINE, February, 1970. (Available from
Fawcett Publications, Inc., New York) *Colored
photographs of decorative papers designed by
Annette Hollander.*

ACKNOWLEDGMENTS

I wish to express my thanks and appreciation to the following people for their contribution toward the development of this book:

Jane Greenfield of the Greenfield Bindery in New Haven, for sharing her knowledge of bookbinding in her course on the subject.

Eva Orsini, artist, craftsman, and teacher, for her encouragement and suggestions at various stages of the writing of this book.

Elaine Silverman, for incorporating these techniques into her high school art curriculum and sharing the discoveries resulting from her teaching.

Jean Rood, junior high school art teacher, for proofreading the manuscript.

Maureen Hollander, for editing the manuscript.

James Hollander, for his technical assistance with the photography.

Carol Hollander, whose hands are shown demonstrating the methods.

Hollander
(5) Design
(